Creatures of the Intertidal Zone

Susan Richardson

Cinnamon Press
Independent Innovative International

Published by Cinnamon Press
Meirion House
Glan yr afon
Tanygrisiau
Blaenau Ffestiniog
Gwynedd LL41 3SU
www.cinnamonpress.com

The right of Susan Richardson to be identified as author of this work
has been asserted by her in accordance with the Copyright, Designs
and Patent Act, 1988. © 2007 Susan Richardson.
ISBN 978-1-905614-16-5
British Library Cataloguing in Publication Data. A CIP record for this
book can be obtained from the British Library

Designed and typeset in Palatino by Cinnamon Press
Cover design by Mike Fortune-Wood from original artwork 'sea
urchin – Towlake' supplied by dreamstime.com

Acknowledgements

Some of the poems included here were previously published in the
magazines *Poetry Wales, The Journal, Poetry Nottingham International,
The Frogmore Papers, Iota, Acumen, Orbis, Envoi, Other Poetry, Obsessed
with Pipework, Peace and Freedom, Earth Love, Raindog, Borderlines. Poetry
Cornwal*, in the anthologies *Contraflower* (Scriberazone 2005), *Dance the
Guns to Silence, 100 Poems for Ken Saro-Wiwa* (Flipped Eye Publishing,
2005), *The Lie of the Land* (Cinnamon Press, 2006) or on webzines: *nth
position, Tattoo Highway, The Hiss Quarterly, Newtopia, Verse Libre
Quarterly, Fail Better, The Scriberazone* and in *Her Mark* (2007 diary
produced by Woman Made Gallery, Chicago)

Printed by Biddles Ltd, King's Lynn, Norfolk

contents

foreword by Ann Drysdale   5

Arctic Blast:

Gudrid the Rare
    1. Arnarstapi, Iceland   13
    2. Greenland   14
    3. Vinland   15
    4. Rome   16
    5. Nun's cell, Iceland   17
Resettlement   18
Ice Pilot   19
Prudhoe Bay   21
The Longest Flight
    1. Restless   22
    2. Atlantic   23
    3. Almost   24
    4. Touchdown   25
Creatures of the Intertidal Zone   26
Inukshuk   28
Kulusuk Cruising   29
Waiting at the Breathing Hole   30
Calving   32
Freydis the Unafraid
    1. Eiriksdottir   34
    2. Evergreen   36
    3. Facing the *Skraeling*   37
    4. Slaughter   39

Warm with Sunny Intervals:

Baggage Claim   43
Phone-call at 4 a.m.   44
This is What Happens When You Let
a Penguin in Your House   45

Defrosting 46
Bookshop Blues 48
Where the Hearth Is 49
Tesco Extra 50
Robben Island: A History 52
African Villanelle 53
Never Forgets 54
Polar Snap 56
Metamorphosis 58
There 60

South Pole Dancing:

Nativity 63
Irritable Bowel Syndrome 65
So long as all you want is a penguin's egg
    1. The Rookery 66
    2. Sweet 68
    3. No Place Like 69
    4. The White Waste 70
Season's Greetings 72
Trial by Ice 74
Aptenodytes Forsteri 77
Grounded 79
Such Crimson Hunger
    1. 87° 32′ South 80
    2. The Pole 82
    3. *The Run Home* 83
    4. Upper Glacier Depot 84
    5. Monument Rock 85
Thought for the Day 86
The Ice is Wearing Purple 88
Three Wives
    1. Mrs Captain Scott 89
    2. Mrs Ernest Shackleton 90
    3. Mrs Edgar Evans 91

Notes on the Text 92

Foreword

Susan Richardson's volume has been at my elbow for several weeks. When I got it I gulped its innards down at a sitting, then regurgitated it later and picked out the tasty bits to swallow all over again. Penguins do that. And I am much more aware of penguin-ness now.

Penguins are just one of several threads that hold this wonderful collection together. It is all about journeys. Some of them are actual, as in the case of the Scandinavian heroines, Gudrid and Freydis, a hundred years apart but sisters in adventure and discovery. The sense of moving forward is underlined by Freydis' feisty belittling of the fortitude of her predecessor. This is how history works. The final sequence dealing with Scott's expedition at the other end of the world is a classic example of this. I shall long remember the description of finding the pole. The snow – and the flag.

The poem that moved me most among these human sequences is "Ice Pilot", which convinced me utterly that this is how it feels to be in charge of a small boat in arctic waters, the power and the fear indistinguishable.

Another sequence deals with the great call of migration, the urgency of going, the desperate need to be elsewhere. Yet another with the journey of evolution. Here was where I gasped loudest at the inventiveness of the poet's vision. For this is where we meet the penguins, whose evolution is upside-down and backwards. In response to their need they have been sucked down a tunnel from the flighted perfection of the migrating bird towards the familiar blubbered, shuffling fleecy creatures. It is suggested that they, like all of us, are still on the road to whatever it is they are destined to become. I was delighted by the idea that the first clumsy landing, the achievement of not-flying was their great defining moment.

Sometimes the lines cross and intermingle; wild animals appear in supermarkets and the gorgeousness of their names glitters in unfamiliar contexts.

One poem is allowed to withdraw from the general theme of wonder and discovery to express rage and disappointment at the earthbound, hidebound shadows of us, who poke and peer and pontificate and have not the soul, the wit to let go and learn. This is the voice of a small gelatinous blob, a creature of the intertidal zone which sends forth small pieces of itself to wreak little vengeances on those who can't be bothered to listen. I admire the poet's restraint in not calling it "An Enemy of the People".

Here is poetry for the most part without obvious form, certainly without overt rhyme, yet each one is driven individually from within into the shape best suited to its purpose. Internal rhyme and assonance, not obvious on the page, sing out when the poems are read aloud, a pleasure I indulged in often. This is free verse at its finest.

Most of the poems in this collection fly without difficulty and I admire them from the ground, but a few of them of them landed especially heavily and I can still feel their impact on my heart.

Ann Drysdale

for Russell
who keeps believing in ice

Creatures of the Intertidal Zone

Arctic Blast

Gudrid the Rare

1. Arnarstapi, Iceland

I know the gasp this grass gives
when it's first touched by snow.

On deep winter nights,
I hear the darkness breathing.

I know the sigh of these cliffs
when the guillemots leave after breeding.

I hear the cry of whales
when their meat is hung to dry
and the shriek of this sky
when fire streams from the mouth of the mountain.

I know each place where this rain's absorbed by the sea,
as after my mother died
when Halldis and Orm
absorbed me.

2. Greenland

They call it the Green Land: it is not green.
Green has gone, along with my innocence.
Each day I replay the terrible scene

of our journey here – my foster parents
seized by the sea, waves snatching them away.
The wind still echoes their screams: I can sense

them everywhere. Faces glacial-grey,
they loom from the gloom of the fog which dwells
throughout this charmless land. I'm told to pray

to some new God, but I'm still drawn to spells.
I'm drawn to Thorstein too. He smiles and oh,
such a strange and perplexing feeling wells

up in me. Like the land I used to know,
I'm all surface ice – but fire burns below.

3. Vinland

The sea which brought us here was calm,
our boat cupped like a gull's egg in a child's palm,
then set down in this nest of sedge and spruce
in this brand-new land

and the sun is a new sun,
stronger than the sun we knew,
bold as the taste of a crowberry

and Karlsefni loves me in a new way
his words soft as *skyr*,
his sperm like buttermilk

and we have a new son,
our Snorri.

There is no need for spells in this new place
where I smell no ghosts,
no need to pray.

Yet still, for my son, I stay on guard
like an arctic tern at Arnarstapi.
I'm ready to dive to fend off threats
and – should it invade this new land –
to peck out the eyes
of Death.

4. Rome

Here, it's easy to believe –
in an honest merchant-God
who trades kind skies for virtuous deeds,
as we gained bright cloth and gold
the year we sailed for home
with our cargo of sagas from Vinland.

Here, my head's free of doubts,
sharp chunks of black lava.

But there, dwells a God who's mad as the sea,
who can take from me husbands,
                    sons,
                    cattle,
                    sheep,
who makes each bush feel pain
at the birth of every berry.

I will mount the horse of my belief
and ride it there
over boggy ground
to face
        Him.

5. Nun's cell, Iceland

My mind, at this time, creaks   like the ice
on mighty   Snaefellsjökull;
like the longboats on which   I sailed
to   the Green Land,   Vinland, Norway, Rome –
and home.

My limbs have   stiffened,
like   Arnarstapi's cliffs,
into basalt   pillars.

Only   my soul is supple
It has   opened,
as the land has split at   Thingvellir,
to entice
God
in.

Resettlement

It's wonderful heavy; that much she knows.
It'll take all the men who are left here
to raise it with that pole, to lift
the lives of its five generations,
the twenty-eight births,
the labour pains ingrained in the wood of its walls,
the nineteen deaths
and all those oilskinned hours
            of waiting
while the men were at sea in a storm.

When her sons talk of leaving,
of living in a place that's not an outport,
her spirit distorts like the limbs
of a spruce in the wind off the water.

There's government money, they say, if she goes,
and so many others have done it,
but her need to leave barely creeps above ground,
stays stunted as bakeapples in the tundra.

So today, instead of cooking up a final scoff,
she boxes the memories she hung to dry and salted,
then stands alone
on the rocks to watch, as they heave
her home onto a raft of casks, rope it
to a boat, set it
            afloat

and ask her
to step   on board.

Ice Pilot

Sometimes, the ice is merely curious. Bergs nose
this boat as cows, on land, crowd
round an unknown rambler. But I like
it more when it acts
aloof, purely for its own amusement. When I ask
it to dance and it refuses.
When sunlit, sequinned, it spins
out of reach, pretending I'm not needed.

I like it, too, when it bucks
and rears, believing it can unseat
the sky. At such times, I'm
the ice whisperer. I must
mesmerise the ice. Guide
its mind and movements. Shift
it at will with a hiss and a whistle. Break
in each berg on a rope in circles.

But I like it best when it stalks
me, snarling. While my audience gawps
from a distance, I permit myself to dream,
for an instant, of being mauled
by the ice. To fantasise
about its bite. Then, with one dismissive flick
of my whip, I force it to slink
to the ring-side.

Did I mention that I also control
the tides? Decide when the glaciers give
birth? Breathe and thus shape
the space around each berg? Decree
when they die? Yes, I'm the one who causes
their collapse. The magnificent crash.

And the silence.

Prudhoe Bay

"I tell you, it sucks. It's a freaking waste-
land. Just shitloads of birds we're not allowed
to shoot. Food's okay and there's a work-out
room, but it's still a real bitch being based
here." "It's awesome. I was, like – wow – amazed
when I first saw that giant pipeline. Proud
too – these fields are the world's cleanest, no doubt
about it, Jesus our Lord God be praised."
Two thousand men work here and hundreds more
come to leer at all the rigs, airports, drills,
roads, wells, waste pits and power plants which gore
the tundra, licking their lips as black blood spills.
The boss, it's clear, has big tumescent plans
to pump it dead with his plump, slickered hands.

The Longest Flight

1. Restless

It begins as a quiver, a twitch
in the black-tinged tips of her wings,
an itch which is quickly relieved
by preening.

It moves to her feet, weaves
its way into the webbing, hovers
in the v-shaped space of her tail.

Soon it permeates everything,
inhabits a layer beneath her skin
like permafrost under the tundra.

As she moults, she hopes the feeling
will go, but each fresh feather she grows
needles her to leave,
before darkness comes in to land
on a brand-new roost of snow.

Her need now beats its wings,
lifts her high,
propels her against
the speckled shell of the sky
till she bursts
    into somewhere
      bigger.

2. Atlantic

This first part is easy.
She's lying, stretched out, on a pillow of wind.
She's how the sky looks when it whistles.

She listens as each filament
from each wise feather's stem
whispers *Keep flying east;*
as the gland at the base of her tail leaks
advice – *Be guided by Polaris.*

She glides above the ancient glacial land
and its shuddering younger neighbour.

When the ocean runs out, she heads
south. Memory tells her not to stay in this place
to which the ice once migrated, extended
its rigid white wings.

3. Almost

Her wings have stiffened. She trudges
through the deep uneven
sky, sinks in drifts and unseen
crevasses, wind-whipped, yet still not stripped
of the will to fly.

For she still trusts the sun,
the golden needle of its compass, the truth
in the unblinking gaze of its eye.

And there's another force which draws her,
causes her to ignore
the land of warmth to her left
where food and rest would be in plentiful supply.

It's a force that's attracted to the North in her,
the thunder of summer light,
the blood of explorers in the tundra,
the tilting cap of ice.

It tugs her towards its itinerant home.
Almost due South,
but not quite.

4. Touchdown

Slowly, she remembers solidity.
The bones of her feet recollect rock,
re-adjust to its touch after treacherous air.

She grows familiar with visibles –
icebergs, plankton, cliffs –
instead of the thread that yanked
her here: the pull of the Pole
and the trans-global route she knew to follow.

She expels a last grey breath of sky, inhales
this continent again, smells
the men for whom it's blank and new,
frostbite on the heel of their need to conquer,
a white tomb.

For her it's the site of summer food,
where her hunger to move
shuts its gaping beak,
shoves its head beneath its wing
and surrenders
                    for a time
to stillness.

Creatures of the Intertidal Zone

Let me set the scene. Life, here in the inbetween,
is dicey. We're exposed twice a day to the sun's

reproachful gaze, accepted – then rejected – by the sea,
stranded, battered, at times all but flattened. Some,

the soft-bodied bivalves, dive into the sand; others cling
to the rocks to withstand the gulls' pecks, the tide's

prising. Me, I specialise in disguise, defy categorisation,
sprout tentacles I claim are petals, create the shape

of a flower where an animal resides. Few land-lubbers
love us: one or two make lampshades from the purple

urchins but most misunderstand us, brand us as eccentric
with our stalk eyes, spines, pulp and suction, with our

spongy undulations, the bladder wrack with battle scars,
the brittle stars and sculpin. From this, you might surmise

that we'd support each other, unite against the censure
of sea, land and sky, but no: though I may hitch a ride

on the back of a hermit crab from time to time, we're all
competing, all both predator and prey. Even that whelk

with her celebrated spiral shell will kill to fulfil her aims.
So why don't I give up, you ask? Seek a low-risk life

out of sight in a deeper ocean; retreat to the splash zone
like the black lichen? Because all the tissue and bristle

of my hollow column body insists I stay. And whenever,
with the frisson of lateral fission, I reproduce, I issue

this one rule: always endeavour to fight, bite back, sting
those rude rock poolers who poke, provoke, grimace

but can't even say my name.

Inukshuk

There never used to be tundra.
In childhood, we grew like blue spruce,
needling outsiders, roots entwined.

But somehow, the temperature dropped over time.
You withdrew, communication got stunted,
and I don't know if you realise, but all that's left
is moss and lichen, a vacant horizon,
a few berries in a bog.

I've turned musk ox – tried scent to get your attention,
and, like an arctic fox, I've grown a new coat each season,
but you still don't seem to see.

So I've decided to build an *inukshuk* in my image.
You'll notice her from a hundred miles away
if you choose to look.
She's the one thing rising
above the permafrost, each resolute rock refusing
to move in even this bitterest winter.

So once you're done with hunting caribou,
or whatever it is you do,
trek for fifty hours to meet her –
don't let your eyes leave her or you'll lose your way.
And when you reach her, read the meaning
in the span of her arms –
This place marks your camp tonight.
At my feet find a food cache.
        Stay.

Kulusuk Cruising

Perfect, I said at the start of the day,
when I hired this tiny boat and the sun was shining,
and the icebergs gleamed like cadets lined up for inspection,
or seemed borrowed from a theatre set, benign as polystyrene.

As I sailed, I saw such striking shapes:
ivory pawns and bishops, a pair of sheepskin slippers,
a giant white chocolate mouse,
Sydney Opera House.

Then, Act Two: the backdrop changed.
The sun slunk off, upstaged by the rain
and the wind screamed till the air turned to splinters,
puncturing my fingers and cheeks.

Now the pawns and bishops are despotic kings.
I'm boxed in – checkmate.
The slippers are a dictator's boots,
the chocolate mouse a wolf
with nine-foot-high incisors.

Clinging to the pitching boat, I listen.
In the Opera House,
the fat lady's starting to sing.

Waiting at the Breathing Hole

The white of this screen burns
my eyes. Its unswerving glare
might well make me snowblind.

There was a time when words would fly
across the screen, like a dog-team speeding,
each at its peak and pulling
equally and all I'd have to do was leap
aboard the sledge, guide it
in the right direction, then
relish the ride.

But suddenly,
            we hit uneven ice.
        Bumped over ridges.
I fell from the sledge.   The dogs fled.
The instructions I yelled
            had no meaning.

So now, with tender eyes,
I must hunt for a hole in the white

and wait

patient

at the rim
for the whiskered nose of inspiration,
for a flippered urge to surge to the surface.

And when it comes, I won't shoot it,
harpoon it   skin it   rip its liver out and eat it raw
leave banners of blood on the snow.

No. I'll feed it all the saffron cod and shrimp it needs,
teach it to move with the ease it knows beneath
the ice

but first, I'll take a few steps back
and just let it

breathe

Calving

They think they're all grown up.
They've had enough of the Greenland glaciers
that have been feeding them for years, so break
off into independent bergs that hang out in Baffin Bay
wondering which direction to take –
and then start drifting.

The open sea can be ruthless, they learn:
most just go with its fickle flow
and only cope by comfort-eating sun,
guzzling its heat and purging themselves
of the very substance they're made of.

By the time they strut past Labrador,
each lusts to become
the most perfect berg on display,
with the best blue-tinged skin,
the glitziest crystals.

And even as they continue to waste,
we say *So beautiful!*
take boat trips for a close-up view,
eschewing the unsightly slob ice
and growlers.

They binge now on our admiration,
strive for a still more striking shape.
They make arches (minimum ice
and maximum space)

while we chip off shards
to add to our drinks,
convince ourselves
nothing's purer.

Once they've limped
to the Grand Banks'
warmer water,
their last chance

to choose resistance
melts, like their flesh,
with a hiss.

Not one has risked
difference.
Not one

has sunk
an unsinkable

ship.

Freydis the Unafraid

1. Eiriksdottir

Thoughts of that bountiful land, where
grapes grow, and trees, and a warm creek
flows, have snagged like knots in my hair.
Beneath this rude cloth, my breasts leak
despair, ache to leave this place, bleak
as all the years that stretch ahead.
I'm worth much more: I'm most unique –
I'm daughter of Eirik the Red.

It angers me blind, like the glare
from the snow, that Gudrid can sneak
her way into favour. Can't bear
it that she, not me, went to seek
that lush land. Shame Thorvard's so weak.
I'll ban him, tonight, from my bed –
then he'll help – a foolproof technique.
I'm daughter of Eirik the Red.

I'd give up my life to go there –
both kids, this hut, each meagre streak
of Luck I've ever known – I swear,
but not by that new god, that meek,
limp, turn-the-other-pallid-cheek
god. I'll swear by the God whose head
holds firm, with a sturdy physique.
I'm daughter of Eirik the Red.

Watch me, Thor – I'll go now to speak
with my brother, beg his ship, spread
the news, raise a crew this same week.
I'm daughter of Eirik the Red.

2. Evergreen

Nothing perturbs me in this perfect land.
Not the grapes that turn men's heads into a flame-streaked sky.
Not the villains from Iceland in my command.

Not the cow that sailed here with us whose milk runs dry.
Not the stench of ill-will that was left
by Gudrid, whose old bed I occupy.

Not being without the children, not these idle breasts.
Not lying, some nights, with Thorvard. Not his hostile attitude
and the way he berates me daily for being immodestly dressed –

for walking barefoot, for failing to raise my snood
over hair that flares like his suspicion. Not the god he's
obsessed with like the rest. Not the *skraeling* that could

attack us, their skin stained as red as desperate pleas.
No, nothing here perturbs me. Except perhaps the trees.

3. Facing the *Skraeling*

Like the smooth head of a seal thrusts
itself through an opening
in the ice, my breast shoved
my shift aside. She sniffed
the air and stiffened
the minute she smelt the hunter, but refused
to cringe or dive.

Instead she dared to confront him, glared
at the bristling tip of his spear
with her defiant pink eye
till his fingers started to quiver
till he lost his grip and took
        flight.

No other woman would have done it.
Gudrid would have run to the hut
with her son. Gudrid would have plunged
beneath her cloak, closed it
over her leaking teats, too feeble
to blunt the hunter.

Yet even though I won, saved
not just myself but others,
they've begun to shun me.
Thorvard, for one, would have rather seen
me pray, plead for succour, scream
his name, would have rather seen
the seal skinned and gutted.

Eirik, alone, would have praised me
and urged me to keep the seal exposed,
not submerge her like this in the frigid ocean.

I can feel her, though, butting
against the ice to create
another hole, waiting
for the perfect moment
        to re-surface.

4. Slaughter

it was easy
easy as saying spells as praying
when you don't believe   as weaving
    then wearing
daring dreams   as squeezing
a grape to separate the seeds
from the stain

it was easy as seizing
rule   as stealing
stored food   as refusing
the woman you once
seduced   as spurning
whoever rescued you

it was easy as felling
every tree   as hacking
with an axe then standing
    back to see
the sap spurt thick and red like
Eirik's hair like
milk from a rare cow like
the Luck I've always lacked

    till now

it was easy as leaving
this bare land   as learning
to forget will be

the black humped back
of memory will dive

        deep

   one flash
of the underside of its tail

then just the jet
           of crimson mist
       which it fitfully   exhales

through the shrivelled skin
   of water

Warm With Sunny Intervals

Baggage Claim

At the airport's large-intestinal tract,
we wait for what we packed yesterday,
conveyer belt contestants from The Generation Game.

Your case emerges first,
slender and stately.
Twenty-eight hours
and not a zip out of place.

My backpack burps and sprawls against a sports bag,
engorged and bored with lack of space.

Never one to drag its wheels,
your suitcase states there's Nothing to Declare.

My backpack waits, knows different.
Its guts are stuffed to bursting and it shows.

Your killjoy case struts off outside.
The carousel lays claim to mine.
I let it spin –
again.

Phone-call at 4 a.m.

Your voice
skindives in me,
dressed in the wetsuit of night.

It swims past my starfish hands,
then rests
on the reef of my spine.

Your voice
keeps that shark sleep at bay,
as it starts
to circle.

It's high tide:
your voice dives low,
prises my oyster open,
finds the pearl.

Your voice
is Jonah,
swallowed whole,
my womb –
the whale.

This is What Happens When You Let a Penguin in Your House

He flippers things into his brood pouch –
your scented candles, couscous,
your Latin jazz CDs – and lays
huge oval needs in their place.
His flat cap and black mac give the illusion
that he's leaving, but he's not
moving – not this, or any, season –
stays squatting on the rocking
floe of your life.

He hunches against your resentment: it swirls
and drifts like snow, but he turns
his back, tucks his bill to his chest,
wills himself not to notice.
You, meanwhile, try to keep
your silver fish alive, your tiny flickers
of freedom. If he ever were to see them,
you know he'd swallow them whole.

Only when he fails to dive
beneath the rigid surface
of your carpet for the tenth successive time
do the drifts begin to shift
from snow to slush.

Only then do you consent
to meet him at the freezer,
and start beaking
the build-up of ice.

Defrosting

The man who brings forth life from ice has left
and there was just one breath
between his last chip and the first   drip drip
from my wing tip –
one breath which bridged my birth and the birth of my death,
one brief breath of perfection.

Those in charge claim they wish to save me.
They pose for photos right beside me,
arms thrown round the shape which was, a moment ago,
my shoulder.
Click click, shiny smiles:
meanwhile, their hands' heat hastens my decay.

I dream of being carved from an arctic of ice,
from a berg so big millennia would bridge my beginning
and my end.
With all my might I visualise white –
so hard I think I'm winning,
                                till drip
                                        drip –
                        my blubber's thinned to nearly nothing.

I'm binge-eating heat against my will –
down goes the blistering pill of the sun with one swallow.
I won't last, you know, much past tomorrow –
if you blinkblink
                you'll miss my shift to liquid
                        from solid.

I resolve though, to dissolve with dignity
to brave the tingles   pins and needles   pain
        as I pass from ice   to space
        till all of me
                flippers to beak   fades to memory,
                till even this
                        begins
                        to
                                drip

Bookshop Blues

I wish I could leave this book's orange spine.
I've been Great Fiction's symbol for too long.
It's time someone thought up a new design –

a parrot, a panda, a porcupine,
Kylie or Kermit or even King Kong.
I wish I could leave this book's orange spine.

I'm sick of James Joyce and Ms Gertrude Stein.
Their prose is a mess, the English all wrong.
It's time someone thought up a new design.

Could make, with my mates, a big chorus line.
Could tap dance down from this shelf with a song.
I wish I could leave this book's orange spine.

The black tie and tails I've got would do fine
(though webbed feet mean I'd just waddle along).
It's time someone thought up a new design.

Let's have 'No Logo' says Naomi Klein.
Let's leave a gap where right now I belong.
I wish I could leave this book's orange spine.
It's time someone thought up a new design.

Where the Hearth Is

Your days were ablaze with ritual –
you knelt at eight to clean the grate each morning,
lit it at twelve,
stoked it at three,
closed the curtains and dragged our chairs close for tea,
then slept with the embers.

I watched with white-hot reverence
as you tossed on more coal,
stirred it up and scorned the guard
that kept in spitting sparks but spoilt our view.

There, you toasted hands
and feet and face and bread,
told flickering childhood tales,
cremated the towels the first time I bled.

And then, I left –
to live in a hut with a man in the snow.
All anthracite, I burned long and slow. He edged
past my guard with more fear than flair,
warned, I suppose, not to get too close
to things that are hot and open.

You, meanwhile, had your hearth torn out
and gas put in,
with simulated flames,
trapped
in the act
of dying.

Tesco Extra

The leopard on the shelf is sleeping, stretched
between the Rice Pops and porridge,
one ear cocked to the endless migrating flock of trolleys.
Two aisles away (I can smell it) she's stashed
a young shelf stacker with a pierced eyebrow
and a punctured throat.
I simply have to have her.
Lugging her into my basket's a real struggle
plus she takes up all the room – but what do humous
and beetroot matter when you've got a cat
with a coat of black roses in permanent bloom?

Next time, in the fruit aisle, I spy
two cheetah cubs and their mother.
She's moving fast but I dive, grab
the swaying j of her tail, drag
her to the till. As the cashier searches
for the bar code, scanning every spot,
I nip back to hunt for the cubs. I can hear,
though not see, them – they're camouflaged
against the bananas but squeaking
like wonky wheels. I don't leave
till I snap them up: two for the price of one.

Three days later, I'm here for the lion
who's sprawled beneath the cheese counter
while heedless shoppers take tickets and wait
for service. As I queue for this alpha male
and some Danish Blue, I soon realise
the rest of the pride's here too – a posse
of females, prowling, and one of them displaying herself,
on heat. The manager – keen, I suppose, to avoid
a copulation scene – lets me have the lot
(as well as a garden umbrella they could use
as a scratching post) for free.

This time, I've only come in for a loaf of bread
but then, between the microwaves
and DVDs I see it – a whole savannah.
Springbok, blesbok, black rhino, kudu,
a dazzle of zebras, a journey
of giraffes, jeeps, tents, cameras, Simon King,
Jonathan Scott... Not till I reach the sign marked
'10 Items Or Less' do I pause
to briefly re-assess. Do I really need those impala?
A velvet monkey screeches over the Tannoy –
Y e s!

Robben Island: A History

1. Exploitation

Men steal penguins' eggs
and guano where they nest. Death
threats in black and white.

2. Isolation

Lepers with too-white
skin and men deemed insane, willed
out of existence.

3. Incarceration

Beaten, they build their
own jail. It's thought that on black
skin, the scars don't show.

4. Evacuation

Penguins saved from oil-
bruised sea are cleaned, restored to
feathered harmony.

5. Reconciliation

The museum proves
that over old wounds, new skin
of many hues grows.

African Villanelle

A swollen tongue of oil invades the sea.
Its kiss is one of death, not of pleasure.
The coast's the throat it probes so ruthlessly.

The Dassen Island penguin colony
feels its urgent, viscous, vicious pressure.
A swollen tongue of oil invades the sea.

They dehydrate and seek shade fruitlessly:
the waterproofing goes from each feather.
Their coat's the throat that's probed so ruthlessly.

Their chicks are fed infected anchovy –
they'll never swim where the water's fresher.
A swollen tongue of oil invades the sea.

Thousands of birds will die, undoubtedly –
the final body count's beyond measure.
The coast's the throat that's throttled ruthlessly.

Amidst all this is one huge irony:
the ship from which it spews is called 'Treasure'.
A swollen tongue of oil invades the sea.
The coast's the throat it probes so ruthlessly.

Never Forgets

Your bone china cup rattles in its saucer.
Your sash window stutters in its frame.
Your whiskey bottle tumbles
from the table and shatters.
That drumming you hear isn't rain.

Skin crinkled like bin bags, they thump
past the cinema (the film burps and judders),
barge past the busker (his dusty dog whimpers
on its string). Cars, that other lumbering herd,
are bumper-to-bumper, as fear flees
to worship at Tesco
or seeks salvation at Esso first.

The gargoyles on your walls wince and shudder
as calves, ancient matriarchs, bulls in musth
stump closer: thousands are now marching
out of town. They've shrugged off
the Maharajahs, bashed
through the bars in the zoos, thudded
from shrunken jungles in their hunt for you.

Crash! – down go your gilded gates –
then each nose, lithe as a petrol pump hose,
uproots an English oak. They tusk
your summerhouse to see if it's edible,
lasso your rococo statues.

Cracks split your ceilings.
Your chimney stacks plummet.
Your stables crumble and they trample
through the rubble, dumping
wrecking balls of dung.

Your door caves in:
they storm straight to your piano
and tear out its teeth without anaesthetic.
One by one.

Polar Snap

Sunday afternoon, late November.
Ducks, puffed up against the wind, huddle
or struggle over grubby bits of bread.
A girl on a Barbie bike
has her hands rubbed by gran to warm them.
Old men in old caps with old dogs on leads
chat by the café that's shut until May.
Perishing, they say, *Can't stand this weather,*
and *Soon be getting dark. Can't abide these long nights.*
Their greatest distaste is saved for the teens
snuggled on the green bench nearby.
He's in just a t-shirt and jeans;
she's on his lap in a tiny skirt,
legs tattooed with cold.
His lips grip hers, their tongues go clubbing.
Other couples, older, snug in coloured fleeces,
walk briskly round the lake.
They're smugly fit, unlike that young mother
who shuffles a hundred yards from her car
to lean on the railing at the lakeside.
Her kids plead for cash for an unseasonal ice cream –
she's too tired to argue,
too tired even to read the plaque
on the memorial lighthouse she's standing next to.

To Captain Scott, it says,
who sailed from Cardiff in nineteen ten
to seek the South Pole
and laid down his life in the Antarctic regions.

What a hero –
to cope with minus thirty degrees
to ski across sixteen hundred miles of snow
to deal with twenty-four-hour nights

to be prepared to leave behind
another young mother,
young wife.

Metamorphosis

To begin with, nothing drastic:
the odd cold bath, air con on max,
the utter absence of shivers.

Then, the skin tingles, each pore forcing
the shaft of a feather forth, like a lid
with a push-through straw.

I go right off garlic, crisps, samosas,
bright red curtains, Gauguin prints.
If I must stay indoors, I want plain
white tiles, a single chilled porcelain sink.

And oh, the fingers. Useless, as if mittened.
And stretched, the tips skimming the floor.
Scissors, chopsticks, forks – all binned.

Breasts blend with belly, waist, hips.
I'm lugging a two-fifty-litre rucksack
in an outsize black wetsuit and wellies.
My tears taste of fish.

Fresh fears keep me from sleeping.
The flecked throats of bull seals.
Ice melt. Oil slicks.

I make a nest from the last
strands in my hairbrush and what I once
knew as pencils, and string.

Soon I must force
this hard new truth between my legs
and hatch it.

There
A Tanka

Here, we use strong soap
to make our bed sheets whiter.
There, the ice sheet breaks,

disintegrates. That's the thing
with white. Always shows the dirt.

South Pole Dancing

Nativity

The night Penguin left his egg,
the sun decided to rise
two months ahead of time

to admire him.
The ozone hole, that rent
in the tent of the southern sky,

miraculously mended.
Leopard seals lost
the will to kill and lolled,

adoring, at Penguin's side.
Even the ice stopped
minding its own business

and paused in its forming.
The Ancient Mariner lowered
his cross-bow; the albatross

remained an auspicious sign.
Scott's frozen corpse twitched
into life – his race for the Pole

with Amundsen was decreed
a dead heat but neither cared,
being more absorbed in reaching

Penguin than competing.
The horizon declared itself more
than a straight line – the meeting

of air and ice curled up at the edges.
David Attenborough arrived to describe
what he saw, but was stunned

as never before, into silence.
And every ordinary penguin
felt a tingle in its wings,

a thawing of primordial memories,
till they soared,
like born-again angels.

Irritable Bowel Syndrome

The ice in my insides is breaking
up. The fracture line runs from rectum
to gut. Hut Point
to the Bay of Whales.

And Scott's in there, stranded,
between his pangs for the Pole and the bloat
of One Ton Depot.

When he left, his finneskoed steps tasted of success.
As I swallowed, he said he was sure he could make it.
But that was before he saw the cracks,
that was before he smelt the penguins.

Scott goes to pot in situations like these.
What I need's an Amundsen to straddle
and subdue the split, to flatten
the *sastrugi*, to leap from berg
to berg, grab each jag of ice
and wrap them in reindeer fur
to stop the stabbing.

And while Scott gripes from his lonely floe,
Amundsen's win will cast a glow in my insides,
will be the glim in the sky
which shows that the ice ahead is solid.

So long as all you want is a penguin's egg

1. The Rookery

In my mitts, is what might turn out to be the missing link
between reptiles and birds.
This, I know I once heard, is a good thing
but I can't think why.
My mind is frozen, and so is the balaclava holding it,
rigid with my breath.

I remember little.
All I know is that darkness is solid and only
the Emperors' brittle cries can inch
through its cracks.

All I know is that our sledge is loaded
with that bully, Cold. It crashes
into the back of our legs, hurls
us into the snow, throws punch
upon punch till our teeth shatter –
it's this utter lack of manners which matters most.

All I know is that no-one else but me and Birdie and Bill
has ever seen this breeding site, yet I still can't tell
what it's supposed to look like.
This yolk that I hold sees more than my broken eyes.

All I know is that for facts about the Emperor's skeletal life
I risk fracturing   mine, as connection
with my feet   and each night's
bony sleep   are already   fractured

I know that   my   heart   slows
that   conversation's iced   over   that   thank you
and please freeze in mid-
air   as soon as they're spoken   and as we march
march   march   collide with the dark
all I know   is I must   stow them   with
this embryo   I grip
in my   mitts

2. Sweet
after Wilfred Owen

With fading hope, like sun fades from this sky
when winter comes, we slog through the snow.
Another frigid march: this time to discover why
the Polar Party failed to return six months ago.
Our hearts are heavier than the loads we drag,
our eyes weighed down by white, half-blind.
Our ponies buckle, even our frayed tents sag
as our thoughts squall and settle on what we might find.

There! There! Look, men – to the west, a shape
like a cairn and what looks like a pair of skis.
At once I'm colder even than at Cape
Crozier. Slowly, we approach – can't really see –
must clear the drifted snow. Dear God. Their tent. What
lies inside? The diaries which each fought to fill.
I pray for a white-out in my mind. Not
always to see them thus. Scott. Birdie. Bill.

If oil had been depoted, and pony meat,
on the Barrier, as an extra store.
If they hadn't had rotten, frostbitten feet.
If he'd not taken five to the Pole, but four.
If Amundsen hadn't got there first –
if he hadn't used dogs but hauled like a man.
If blizzards weren't raging (for nine days, the worst).
If there'd been extra hoosh and pemmican...
Success with the eggs now feels like defeat,
but hardest of all to understand
is the lie so many now speak: that it's sweet
to die for your native land.

3. No Place Like

T h i s l i f e
doesn't fit. When
I try to stand up, I crack
my head, have to stoop like
I've got igloo-back. It used
to fit well, like my hands fit my
mitts, but since my British Museum
trip, it restricts every movement. I
took them the eggs – said 'Three men
nearly died for these' – but they might as
well have refused them. Then I asked a
man whose scales will never evolve into
feathers whether I could have a receipt
but he treated me with the heedlessness
of snow. So now, as I go about each
day, I'm three men packed into a
two-man tent, two men crammed
inside a sleeping bag for one,
one penguin on shrinking
ice far from its rookery,
trying to hatch
a rock.

4. The White Waste

The crevasse I've fallen into is deep and wide.
I'm dangling by my harness still.
My head is an egg that's cracked and fried
but soon I'll be rescued by Birdie and Bill.

I'm dangling by my harness still
in this godforsaken trench of ice.
But soon I'll be rescued by Birdie and Bill
from thoughts that gnaw like rats, that swarm like lice.

In this godforsaken trench of ice
do I smell frozen sweat or mustard gas?
Were there rats that gnawed and swarming lice?
Those years near the Pole are themselves a crevasse.

Do I smell frozen sweat or mustard gas?
Do I hear ponies' screams or men's manic laughter?
Those years near the Pole were themselves a crevasse
between my youth and the white waste hereafter.

Do I hear ponies' screams or my own manic laughter?
Even the pus in my blisters has frozen.
Between my youth and the white waste hereafter
a battle was fought I now wish I'd not chosen.

Even the pus in my blisters has frozen –
they bulge on my feet like Emperors' eggs.
I fight in a battle not willingly chosen –
first frostbite, now gangrene, first toes and now legs.

They bulge on my feet like Emperors' eggs –
one for each man who needlessly died.
First frostbite, now gangrene, first toes and now legs.
The crevasse I've fallen into is deep and wide.

Season's Greetings

This sky is heavier than fear of a predator
and she's the only one holding it up, the only
one being systematically crushed – beak bites
into breast, but she's too scared to move lest
she drops it, lest it shatters into a billion pieces
of night, and everyone will blame her – *so clumsy* –
and how will she mend it, and for everything to be
so relentlessly black she must already have made
a serious blunder. She feels responsible for the stars,
dreads hearing them scream as they smash onto
the ice, frets the moon will bruise, fears it won't
bounce, or if it plunges into the sea, can the moon
swim? might the moon drown?

Worry blizzards and accumulates –
but just when she knows she can't shoulder
the sky for a moment longer,
it begins to lift
and lighten.

Relief rises to warm her.
She raises her head and stretches
to the rhythm
of the ebbing ice,
rejoices, with each movement,
in the buoyancy of blue.

Soon, she's belly-sliding too,
gliding towards the lucid horizon
till suddenly –

Stop.
Someone's watching.

The sun's censorious eye
is fixed on her. Constantly.
Burning holes in whatever she chooses to do,
in her effortless future.

She swerves behind a berg, dives
down a crevasse but the sun roots
her out every time.

Finally, she stoops. Offers
the shelf of her back. Begs
the sky to descend again
and lie there.

Trial by Ice

He wishes the ice would disguise
its indifference.

One night, he thought he heard
the ice crying
but
        slipped
on the surface of its silence.

He pecks at its self-reliance,
says he'll help it to adapt
to the fact that it's shrinking
but it
        spits
spiked sticks of denial.

He tries to hatch
a new zest for life for the ice
but the ice yawns
and the egg
        falls
down the crevasse.

He pledges his penguin love to the ice,
wants to surprise the ice
with the strength
of his clumsy, blubbery desire,
but it
        shrugs
him into the sea.

He squats heavily on and crushes
the ice, he kicks the ice, he sicks up
yesterday's krill on the ice.
He hunts with such skill that he kills the ice
but the ice just goes on
lying there
        being
white.

Aptenodytes Forsteri

i

This will make my name: this nose-stone, this rude
Carving, this shark-teeth bracelet, these Ear-sticks,
This mourning-dress of feathers from the tails
Of Tropick-birds. Though Cook still has not found
His Great South Land, though each man aboard this
Stinking ship behaves exceeding crude, though
I crave rare food, having sickened of dry
Biscuits, I have catalogued all of these
Curiosities. Each is bound to the
String of my name like bones to this Necklace.

ii

This, too, will make my name: Cook, frozen with
Gut pain as the ship noses through the ice.
The Surgeon, Patten, nurses: I return
To my cabin, aft, to attend to my
Catalogue. And there I find him – Cook's dog
(Most detestable) gnawing the carved Club
(Most prized) I acquired on the Friendly Isles.
There is only one remedy. And thus,
Tonight, it comes to pass that Cook is served
Meat Broth – and eats. Saved. By Johann Forster.

iii

I have tired of his search for the Great South
Land. I have tired of this Cold which takes my
Joints in its jaws and bites. There is naught for
Me to do in these High Latitudes but
Sketch those strange Bird-fish (enormous, black and
White, raucous as the men with whom I'm here
Confined) on an ice-caked page which my quill
Can scarce penetrate. Let us sail north to
Warmer isles, where I may eat fresh pig, where
The sun may make some new scheme germinate.

iv

I have laboured a year to forge these words –
Unadorned with Mother of Pearl, tassels
Of feathers, bits of Coco-nutshells – pure,
Scientific, plain. Cook will publish his
Account of our voyage and it will be
Thought exceeding fine – but then will come mine.
It will be a sturdy collier bark,
Holding the coals of Scholarship, gliding
On a wide sea of fame. And high above
The waterline, writ large, will be my name.

Grounded

Some would say it's evolution in reverse,
this learning to unlearn,
weaning myself off the wind, spurning
my strongest instinct.
But as far as I'm concerned, there's a freedom
in not remembering, even wider
than the freedom of the glide.

I confess the process hasn't been easy –
willing myself not to rise, stilling
my wings, forbidding
each feather to yield
to its urge for air.

First, I focused on not trusting
I wouldn't fall –
the sky, after all, has never been that supportive.
It's mostly flat and grey – plain bored –
has never embraced me in the same way as water.

I next progressed to failing to navigate,
doubted the reliability of the sun,
turned best-loved bergs, from above, into strangers.
I acquired a real flair for plummeting,
and still rate my first bungled landing
as the greatest achievement of my life.

From there, it was a small step
to gaining blubber,
to my wings becoming stubbier,
to flapflap   stutter,
jump   only to
                 slump
stomach-down
on the ice.

It's quite a relief, not having a technique
that everyone envies.
Even walking's a challenge these days.
Perhaps, in time, I'll unlearn that too.
Perhaps I'll persuade
my black hunched back to hatch
the beginnings
of a fin.

Such Crimson Hunger

1. 87⁰ 32′ South

He picked me because I'm the biggest,
because I'm the strongest,
because I can drag myself and the sledge the furthest –
that's why he picked me.

I've never been ill in all my life –
unless you count the nights of drink
and the tiny cut just here on my hand
(and I only got that from mending the sledge
and even now it's healing).

It was me or Crean. He picked me
because I'd been to sea with him before
and skied eleven hundred miles
on the voyage of the 'Discovery'.
I slept in a bag with him,
fell in a crevasse with him –
that's why he picked me.

He said it was meant to be
four men, not five, marching to the Pole.
He said it was meant to be
four men, not four men and me.
But he knows I can fight the cold. He knows
I can defeat the white with purple curses.

Taff – Seaman Evans.

Sir?

He picked me.

2. The Pole

Just a red flag with a blue-and-white cross
and snow

and snow

and snow

and so
our noble race

is lost

3. The Run Home

My hand is quite okay, sir.
Yes, I'm quite okay.

I just feel such crimson hunger.
My ribs are what's left of that rotting ship,
wrecked in Rhossili Bay, stuck
in the sand for dogs to piss on.

He picked me because I'm the biggest.

16 ozs biscuits
12 ozs pemmican
3 ozs sugar cubes
2 ozs butter
a day.

4. Upper Glacier Depot

In the tent tonight, Dr. Wilson stops writing his diary
to examine my hand,
examine my face,
examine my feet.

He tells me my nose has gone
but I still smell white.
He tells me my nails have gone
but white is still trapped beneath them.

I must clean them, clean them,
mustn't let him see them,
must try a new tongue to change the meaning
eira
newynog
gwyn

5. Monument Rock

I've climbed down Rhossili's cliffs – they told
  me I slipped, but sir, I'm
     quite
fine.   I've reached the beach now – I'm
  waist-deep
    in sand.
       I'm making castles, taking
my gloves off to shape them,
            with a stranger's
  hand.
Lois and the children are here now –
  four figures rising
from the white waves.   Look – I've built you
  a castle. Look –
  it'll never   collapse
or   rot.   Look –
     I'm   planting
     my flag
      in
     the
       top

Thought for the Day

God's improbable.
God's that deep ocean life which thrives
beneath the Ross Ice Shelf,
though deprived of air and sunlight
like those thoughts we dare not recognise.

God's totally white
and god's the krill-rich penguin shit which stains
the white pink.

God's the chick which will die, if it leaves
its parent's pouch, in under a minute.
God's the blubber that keeps this parent alive:
god can swim in seas of forty degrees Fahrenheit
and survive.

God's the leopard seal skulking at the ice's limit
which mauls all penguins that try to dive
across the border into water.

God's gone outside and may be some time.
God's died in a blizzard and has risen
again in Ranulph Fiennes.

God spouts misty lies from the blow-holes of orcas.
God's sold his soul to the South Magnetic Pole
and won't quit shifting.

God is getting hot. Big chunks
of god keep breaking off.
God will force the waters of the world to rise –
and he'll capsize much more than a lone Pacific atoll

for god knows that most people have stopped
believing
in ice.

The Ice is Wearing Purple

Being cold was once a thrill, but now I'm old
I've lost the will to aspire to a record minus.

I'm so old I remember when penguins could fly
and swallow the stars, like the sky swarmed with krill.

My skin has wrinkles big enough
for entire expeditions to fall into.

I've had my fill of fighting the sun, of his summers
of abuses – each part of me that meets

the sea's been bitten ragged. I'm also tired
of getting blamed for the deaths of the men

whose footprints scar my face – my being white,
it seems, gives people leave to colour

me in with their own mistakes
and failings. So now, as I approach my final

melting, I've no urge to think of quenching
the thirst of the world. Instead, I dream of sinking

every nation, hearing History splutter as it goes under,
sweeping all the years of myth and bluster away.

Three Wives

1. Mrs Captain Scott

What do I know of cold?
Clay before I start to mould it.
Untold rows of unfinished heads.
You, my marble marvel.
Your side of the bed.

2. Mrs Ernest Shackleton

He says he'll never go South again.
He's home for good. And I quote:
May you never know cold as I did, my love –
I want you to have this new coat.

He owes his men two years' wages –
all those who chose to devote
themselves to his Southern journey.
I suppose I was owed a new coat.

His map's inscribed with women's names –
mountains, glaciers, the boat
that sailed to Elephant Island.
My name's sewn into this coat.

He'll be long gone come September.
Like the land, he'll seem stark and remote.
His skin will be glazed with a layer of ice.
Mine won't.

3. Mrs Edgar Evans

Blizzards of brave words
drive you to the Pole. I wait
in ice-blue silence.

Notes on the Text

Gudrid the Rare: Gudrid is one of the most intrepid women in world history. She was born in Iceland in the late tenth century, moved to Greenland and later undertook a sea journey to Vinland (believed, by some, to be Newfoundland). Here, early in the eleventh century, she gave birth to the first European in North America. Later travels took her to Norway and on a pilgrimage to Rome before she finally returned, as a nun, to Iceland.

Freydis the Unafraid: Freydis Eiriksdottir, another audacious tenth/eleventh century female Viking, was born in Greenland. Frustrated by her illegitimate and lowly status, she succeeded in organising an expedition to Vinland, which was rich in both grapes and timber. When threatened by a *skraeling* (aboriginal inhabitant of Vinland), she allegedly responded by baring her breast, causing him to flee. The expedition ended in a massacre, which she reputedly instigated, following months of dissent among the Norse settlers.

Defrosting: South Korean environmental artist, Byung-Soo Choi, specialises in sculpting penguins from blocks of ice, which he then leaves to melt outside Parliament buildings and at international environmental conferences.

Never Forgets: Musth is a condition of bull elephants associated with heightened testosterone production. They secrete a tar-like substance from a gland between the ear and eye and become aggressive.

So long as all you want is a penguin's egg: **The White Waste:** Apsley Cherry-Garrard was the youngest man to accompany Scott to the Antarctic. In 1911, he went on a harrowing winter journey in search of Emperor penguins' eggs with Bill Wilson and 'Birdie' Bowers, both of whom died some months later on Scott's ill-fated expedition to the Pole.

Aptenodytes Forsteri: Johann Forster was the naturalist who accompanied Captain Cook on his 1772-75 expedition to the South Seas. He is remembered today for having been one of the first people to sight and sketch the Emperor Penguin: hence its scientific name *Aptenodytes Forsteri.*

Such Crimson Hunger: Monument Rock: Born on Gower and brought up in Swansea, Edgar Evans was one of the four men to accompany Captain Scott on his 1911-12 trek to the South Pole. They were beaten to the Pole by Amundsen and Evans was the first of Scott's party to die, from a combination of starvation, injury and exhaustion.

Cinnamon Press
Independent Innovative International

We hope you have enjoyed this book from Cinnamon Press.

Cinnamon publishes the **best in poetry, fiction and non-fiction**.

For writers – bi-annual competitions in four genres – first novel, novella, short story & first poetry collection. Cash prizes and publishing contracts.

For book lovers - great poetry and fiction titles from the best new names as well as established writers.

For the best amongst poetry journals: *Envoi* – celebrating 50 years of poetry

For a full list of titles visit:

www.cinnamonpress.com

Cinnamon Press

Independent Innovative International

Cinnamon Press Writing Awards:

Four writing competitions with two deadlines each year for: Debut Novel; First Poetry Collection; Novella; Short Story

Deadlines June 30th and November 30th

All entries by post + sae & details - name, address, email, working title, nom de plume.

Novel: 1st prize - £500 + publishing contract. Submit 10,000 words. 5 finalists submit full novel & receive appraisal. Fee: £20 per novel.

Poetry Collection: 1st prize - £100 & contract. Runners up published in anthology. Submit 10 poems up to 40 lines. Three finalists submit further 10 poems. Fee: £16 per collection, includes copy of winners' anthology.

Novella: 1st prize - £200 + contract (20 - 45,000 words). Submit 10,000 words. Four finalists submit full novella. Fee: £16 per novella.

Short Story: 1st prize - £100 & publication. 10 runners up stories' published in winners' anthology. Length 2,000 - 4,000 words. Fee: £16 per story, includes winners' anthology.

Entries to: Meirion House, Glan yr afon, Tanygrisiau, Blaenau Ffestiniog, Gwynedd, LL41 3SU. Full details:

www.cinnamonpress.com